Tales from the Sexy Poet

Tales from the Sexy Poet

To Have Loved & Lusted

By Viola Davies

Published by The Sexy Poet

Published by The Sexy Poet
Camp Springs, Maryland
Printed in the United States of America

ISBN 978-0-692-70431-8

Dedication

This book is dedicated to those whose presence in my life provided content, to MFJ who told me I should write it all down, and to my strong, independent mother who raised a strong, independent daughter.

Foreword

I have attempted to do something epic at the end of my adult decades. I grew up in New York City riding public transportation, so for my nineteenth birthday I got my driver's license. For my twenty-ninth birthday I got a tattoo. For my thirty-ninth birthday, I got on stage in front of a crowd of people and recited *I've Had Good*. This book was born that night.

To Have Loved

To Have Lusted

To Have Loved

Self-Love

Not broken, but fractured, just limping along,
won't stay down long enough to let it heal.

Building scar tissue and new tough skin,
won't let anything grow there again.

How many planted areas are now barren?
No water from tears; no dried petals of lost love.

Just a wasteland of heartbreak,
waiting to be recovered,
left undiscovered by lover after lover.

My heart of holes is whole,
strong and resilient;
a force of my nature.

I know of no other way than to,
keep moving forward day after day.

Don't cry for me, I don't cry for myself.
This soul I expose is my gift to me.

Me letting you in is so others will see,
that it is indeed possible to lose in love
and still be a winner.

Nothing makes me feel less than,
because I have a foundation on which to stand.

I love myself in all of my magnificence;
with or without a man.

That isn't something I say to convince
you, me, or them.
It is fact that my splendor is only
a reflection of him.

If you know the him that I am speaking of,
then you know I speak the truth.

The ability to reveal myself like this,
Is my gift from above.

So sit back, relax and enjoy.
This is my labor of love.

The Heart is the Home

I opened the door to my heart
and you walked in
and made yourself at home.

You made it known
that you were not just visiting.

You unpacked;
hung art;
forwarded the mail;
rearranged the furniture.

You began to take up residence,
so I gave you a key,
the master key,
and as you toured your new home,
you opened doors locked long ago.

You happened in my life
and joy flowed
and I realized at that moment;
I love you.
You now live in my heart.

The Courage to Love

You will break each other's hearts

You will tell each other lies big and small

You will be selfish, for the ego of "I"
will sometimes want to win above "We"
and you will acquiesce

You will be hard when the other needs you to be soft

You will make excuses for your own shortcomings
and for your mate's

You will forget important dates, places, and events

You will be late, often, shattering
the other's peace of mind

You will sometimes want more and sometimes want
less and at either time your mate will want the
opposite

You will go to bed angry and wake up angry and be
angry all day

You will not kiss on angry days, you will not hug,
and you will not express the love hidden beneath the
anger

You will overemphasize the smallest thing
and completely miss the biggest thing

You will ignore when you need to pay attention
You will trip and stumble but not fall because
You will be there to catch each other

All of these things that scare people away from love
will happen but it is the fact that you choose to love
in spite of the fear that makes love worth it.

You will be responsible
for holding each other's heart

You will choose honesty
because it really is the best policy

You will let go of the urge to be selfish
because you have someone to share your life with

You will soften your hard edges for your mate's sake
You will have no need for excuses, only actions

You will remember anniversaries, birthdays, the
place you had your first kiss, and that time you got
lost on a walk

You will make every effort to be on time because you
know how it feels to be the one waiting

You will continue to want more and sometimes want
less but you will compromise so that your mate
wants the same not the opposite

You will not go to bed angry,
you will kiss and make up

You will show love,
because you know love is valuable

You will not miss the big things or the small things,
You will love through all things

You will not ignore,

You will pay attention

You will not fear,

You will have the Courage to Love

Weak Love

Your love was a weak lie you told me from the start

How could you have been telling the truth when

You didn't love yourself enough to fully love me

You were everything I knew a man could be

Until you weren't

You said all the right things

Did all the right things,

Until you didn't

You lied over and over again

With every stated I love you

Because that was your weak way

You said marry me so I made space for you in my life

We were set to be husband and wife

Had me designing rings and picking out a dress

But you told lies of omission

I found out when you left

I was not the damsel in distress you needed me to be

So when she called, you galloped off to her rescue

Leaving me in the dust

Wondering what happened to us

Your weak love cracked my heart; broke my trust

The worst part is that you don't seem to know

How much better your life could have been

How much more you deserve

Than to continue being used by everyone

Trying to bleed you dry

You just keep passing along the lies

From them to you to me, where will it end

When will you figure out that you are worth more

Than the lies you have been told

By the souls that have already been sold

When will you return to the man I once knew

Instead of this boy who lies in love

Because he needs to be accepted

When will you stop giving out this weak love

And stand in your strength

When baby, when?

That Kind of Love

Your love was just never enough.

I deserved more than you were giving.

I wanted more than you were offering.

I demanded more from what you were saying.

We had love but I was the only one loving.

Noun and verb are both required.

The noun without the verb and we are just friends.

The verb without the noun and we are just lovers.

I want a friend and lover not one or the other.

I deserve the kind of love that writes songs.

Not just love but admiration and adoration.

The kind of love that makes your heart smile.

Give that Barack look at Michelle,

That Ossie look at Ruby Dee; kind of love.

Not lust, but longing,

Not a desire to taste but savor me, kind of love.

The kind of love that makes you want to,

meet my parents.

And say thank you.

That kind of love would be enough.

The Wait of Love

I am afraid of my heart breaking from the weight of
the love I feel. How do I hold on and let go at the
same time? I don't want to hold anything back; I
want to give almost everything, except the part of me
I only want to share with…me. I want to keep me,
keep him, and keep us. I want to travel with him and
alone. I want to belong to him and to no one. I want
to be with him and without him at times.

Why am I Velcro? Why can't I be more like crazy
glue? Or maybe painter's tape; it holds well but
leaves no mark when you pull it off. I walk lightly,
he stomps, we leave footprints all over each other's
bodies. We walk in each other's shoes. I learn him
but miss my shoes. I want to jump in, one toe at a
time. He is patient but he won't hold his heart
forever. He wants to give it to me and I want him to
wait.

Just a few more kisses till I'm sure. A few more
candlelight dinners and after dinner walks. A few

more plans for the future, a few more doors opened, and chairs pulled out.

Just a few more nights like this when he looks at me like that and I feel like I never knew what it felt like to be loved by a man until now.

There is no more love to wait for, all of it is here, right now, and the weight of it is the feeling that I've been missing all this time.

Unspoken Vows

When I first saw you, your soul greeted mine,
and in a short time you showed me,
that my soul would be safe with you.

I knew then that we would be here now.
That feeling of being right where you belong,
is why we are standing here today.

It's not just about our big love,
it's about knowing ourselves,
Enough to know that we belong together.

I feel that every good and not so good day.
So I need you to know that:

I vow to love you even when I don't like you.
We will get on each other's nerves.

I vow to catch you,
even if I'm the one who made you fall.
I will trip you but never on purpose.

I vow to be there for you,

even when I'm away,

I will support you from afar.

I vow to take the blame,

even when I've done nothing wrong.

If you hurt, I'm sorry.

I vow to care,

even when I'm being careless with your heart.

I will not take you for granted.

I vow to always try,

because we both know I'm not perfect.

I will make mistakes.

Please choose forgiveness.

I vow to laugh at your jokes,

even when they're not funny.

Let's always choose laughter.

All these things I vow to be to you and for you.

Our histories have brought us here

for today is when our roads merge.

Today I become your wife and,
receive you as my husband.

Today, I proclaim to you and to all,
that I lay claim to your heart.

I love you just isn't enough to explain,
So I am professing, proclaiming,
and confirming, to the world,
that my heart, my love, and my soul,
belong to you.
I am yours.

With every hug, kiss, and soulful exchange I promise
to make you feel no less than the joy you feel right
now for the rest of our eternity.

My love, our love, one love, forever.

Four days after the wedding

I love you more than you will ever know

Wherever you take your heart, mine will go

Wherever on this planet you go to belong

My heart will always be along

This heart will always beat for you

I hope you know that is true

No distance can come between

What your love of me now means

For I have now been truly loved

The way that love was designed from above

The original plan between human and human

It matters not if it be man and woman

I love all of you, my beloved one

Under the palest of moon and brightest of sun

Our love has no end or beginning, it is a perfect ring

This unbreakable bond we have is the real thing

So don't say goodbye, my love will never be far

I will get to you as fast by plane, or train, or car

One word from you and I am on my way

I will drop whatever I am doing that day

Nothing is more important than being there for you

I know you feel the same way too

So go and take care of what you must

You absolutely have my trust

I know you'll be coming back stronger than before

I will be here waiting for you right inside the door

To rejoin the body to the heart you take when you go

They took you away and buried you deep,
while I was still screaming no.

There is not a single part of me,
that does not miss your voice,

The do-gooders urge me to move on,
as if I have a choice.

My heart is broken in a million pieces,
I am trying my best,

I will love you forever my heart,
in peace may you rest.

Desperate Love

He wasn't everything I wanted, but at the time,
just what I needed.

A gentle giant to soothe my savagely wounded beast,
a calm to my storm that made the winds whisper in
reverse.

He heard my silent screams and came running to my
rescue, not realizing that he was the one who would
need to be saved,
from me.

I was drowning in despair; he jumped into the
quicksand of my life. We held onto each other too
tight to breathe.

This osmotic relationship consumed us both and
soon we were lost at sea, until we discovered a
direction, and gained a passenger. We now had a
reason to survive.

The storms continued to whip us hard. We took
desperate measures to retain our course and right
our ship. We steered in yet another direction to
calmer seas, obtaining a second passenger. We were
good. We thought we could survive.

But our survival was temporary. The sea was too choppy. Hearts could not be unbroken. Trust could not be restored.

Soon there was nothing left to save except the creations of the love that once was nothing less than everything.

We were desperate to love more, desperate to connect more, desperate to understand more, to be more, to care more, more, more until the tsunami of desperation tore us apart and washed us up on the shore of our lives, tired, weary, wounded and damaged.

Our love did not survive our desperation and it, along with our dreams and potential, went out with the tide.

Championship Match

So young when we first fell in love.

We had no idea what we were doing.

Playing house and doing things,
how we thought we should.

Living a life where we "should" on ourselves
repeatedly.

Because we should have done this,
and we should have done that.

Nothing organic, nothing authentic,
because we had no idea,
how to be husband or wife.

We just kept fighting to keep our love alive.

We just kept fighting to not let it fall apart.

We just kept fighting, always each other,
and never together.

We were the heavyweight champions of love,

Fighting back the naysayers with every kept vow.

But when our marriage was on the ropes,
every move was a potential count out.

Throwing punches,
because we didn't want to let divorce win.

Hoping and praying that wasn't our destined end.

Taking off and coming back because of the ring.

We danced around and stayed on our feet,
for as long as we could.

But no matter how hard we fought,
it just wasn't meant to be.
We couldn't get up from the mat.

On fight night, we were bruised beyond repair.

It was a double knockout.

The crowds showed up celebrating our demise.

He went to his corner, I went to mine.

The Game

You're hurting me,
I keep letting you,
over and over again

In this masochistic game we play,
I wager my heart,
you always win.

Giving what I can't live without,
yet you don't care that I share.

You take it and break it,
but with yours you fake it.
Daily treating mine with scorn,
I simply band aid the pieces that have been torn.

Don't know why I keep letting you hold,
What you don't cherish and leave out in the cold.
Submissive master of my own disaster
This cycle is happening faster and faster

Somehow I believe I deserve the pain
Because I keep coming back again and again
Can't stop wanting what doesn't want me in return
Damn, I keep letting myself get burned

O Hell, now here we go again.
With me just letting you win.

Why won't I stop playing this painful game?
When our situationship has been given no name.

In my mind, it just takes time,
For you to give me what should already be mine.

I love you

You could love me,
but you won't let me in.

So I stay,
so easily convinced by men,
Who say the next time around,
will be my turn to win.

Broken Heart Restart

At first, I couldn't get out of bed

Lingering on life-support but refusing to be dead

In and out of my broken-hearted comatose state

Questioning every choice I made too late

Wondering where I went wrong

Crying while listening to sad songs

Wasting away and losing pounds

Waiting for my body to be found

Seeing the visitors come and go

Reminding me to use this change to grow

Pointing out that his love held me down

Can't lay here in my sorrows and drown

Yes I have a broken heart

I need a defibrillation restart

I am now bounding out of bed

Getting my heart right, starts with my head

Just because this is no longer his home

Does not mean that I have to be alone

Getting my life back with friends around

My heart is on the rebound

I see that handsome man over there

He's been waiting for me for a year

No longer a sad flower on the wall

Maybe I'll finally return his call

And even if he's done waiting for me

There are plenty of fish in the sea

Independent Woman

I am an independent Woman

So listen to me when I say

I don't need you to pay my bills;

maintain my car;

fix my life; or

provide for my children.

I don't need you to give me career advice;

handle my business; or

treat me like I'm weak, and

I don't need you to fight my battles.

But

I do need you to pay me compliments;

maintain our connection;

fix me dinner sometimes; and

provide for our future.

I do need you to give me your heart;

handle your fan club; while

treating me with respect; and

I do need you to fight,

for us

Because

I don't need you.

I want you.

But I will not chase you.

I am a jewel to be discovered.

So I'm just going to sit here on my throne,

Until you recognize the truth.

When you figure out that the Queen,

Protects the King,

You'll stop playing with these pawns.

You and I

You throw yourself at me
because you know you will be caught.

I have never let you down; you know I never will.

You don't take advantage of my love just because
you know that, I'll always have your back.

You know the world man built,
was not designed to let you be great.

I will keep you secure and always be,
your safe place to land.

You can count on me to not let you fall,
and never drop the ball.

You are your own worst enemy,
and often need to be rescued.

I will come running to save you from yourself.

You will never do enough,
to make me love you more or less,
as long as you continue to give your best.

You are never satisfied with what you already have.

I will forever support you in obtaining your goals.

You recognize that everything you desire,
will not take you higher.

You continue to make efforts,
even though my family says you're using me.

I know you better than they do,
plus I'm the one using you.

You give me everything, every piece of you,
the love I know is true.

You're leaving me because you have to grow.
I have no regrets, our relationship has run its course.
You are the best person I've met in years,
The reality of your absence brings me tears.

Fairytale

Once upon a time there was a beautiful woman,
living in her pretty prime.

So much so that there were plenty of men
standing in her line.

She was the prize of the long journey they were on,

To find her, to win her, to make her the one.

So many wanted to be her mate,
that they were willing to wait weeks for a first date.

Offering her delicacies and extravagant events,
mistakenly thinking it was the path to her heart.

Though competition proved them worthy opponents,
they weren't very smart.

For this queen needed much more than a prince;
she needed and desired a king.

A man fit to lead, direct, and protect her
and her beautiful heart.

To provide care and comfort,
in sickness and in health,

A king designed for this particular queen.

A man of reality, not just of a dream.

She was ready for more than any could handle,

Most of them just did not have the stamina.

To love this queen in all of her glory,
was more than any man had imagined.

So they stepped forward, one by one
and professed their undying love,

But as she cycled through the line,
she could not find the best.

Because none, not even one,
could pass her simple test.

Could you, would you, forsake all others,
everyone, yes even your mother?

That, the men just could not do,
it seems saying you want it
does not make it true.

The queen however refused to play second fiddle,
and the men were unhappy being caught in the
middle.

Love she said is not the same as devotion.

It is perhaps, a singular emotion,
that which require others to support its success.

The right man who is king,
will understand all of this,

So for now she chooses to be single,
the pretty Queen of hearts,

Continuing to add King candidates to the line,
having fun and sharing laughter

Waiting, searching, and open to love;
hoping for her happily ever after.

Riddle

It makes me happy, makes me sad
Sometimes it can make me go mad

I feel it way down in my soul
Even when I lack it, I still feel whole

I can give it but can't take it
It's amazing when I can make it

Take care to not share it with too many
Or diseases you will likely have a plenty

There will be times when it is taken away
Even though you really want it to stay

This is when you should give it to you
To make your desire for it renew

'Cause there's nothing better than being in deep
With a partner willing to take the leap

Although there's the extra tax you pay
So together you can legally lay

If you treat it like it's sacred to receive
You may insure that it will not leave

It will heal your pain, and calm your stress
It will make your daily worries seam less

When it is good, it may still make you cry
That is the truth, it does not lie

It will protect you from getting burned
If it is always being returned

Making it will help you create it over 9 months long
And in that time it will grow tenfold strong

What is this magic I speak so intelligently of
Yes you guessed it, of course, it is love

All for One

No longer out here playing these games for fun,

I gave them all up for the one.

I had to move fast to shut it down,

Because he was not playing around.

Those boys no longer had a chance at the dance,

When the real man showed up with a plan in hand.

The one I was not searching for walked in like a boss.

And I was at a loss,

To explain to the others they were no longer required,

Now that the one, was finally interviewed and hired.

He breathed into me and that was all it took,

For me to not have to take another look,

At another one for the rest of my life,

I am going to end up being this man's wife.

He made his intentions clear from the start.

His words, like cupid's arrows, straight to my heart.

So farewell my many lovers of old,

Announcements have been sent, you have been told

My dating game used to be all the way live, but,

This is it, game over, the Game Changer has arrived!

Always Love

I don't always like him but there is always love.

After so many years of him owning my heart,
love is always there.

Even after the heartbreak, the pain, the suffering,
and the judgment; there is always love.

Some days he is an ass and so am I.

Some days I miss my friend.

I know this strange relationship we have,
will never end.

Till death do us part is what I said in my head.

His wellness still matters to me till this day.

In sickness and in health I promised to myself;

Even when I am tired and wish he would go away.

The Universe heard and I'm moving hundreds of
miles today.

I'll miss him from afar.

My frenemy is gone, now what do I do with this love
I ask?

I give it always to our collective contributions;

Lasting reminders of the love that once was, still is,
and will always be.

We were ready to say I do but now we don't.

He still lives in my love Universe, orbiting my moon,
creating rare and unusual eclipses.

We scream and shout at the train station and
months later meet for drinks.

He a part of me and me a part of him.

No use in fighting the truth that is;

There will always be love.

He has loved others since and so have I;

It matters not to what is between us.

There is always love, stronger than hate and more
powerful than indifference.

Through the madness, the fear,

the pride before the fall,

I know it for sure that love conquers all.

This knowledge does not make me weak,
it makes me whole.

This love is a part of who I am.

I accept it, fighting to reject it,
brought me nothing but pain.

Now I love someone and I give him the benefit,
of all my heart has learned.

He knows I will always love him.

Long Love

The decades have changed,

The way we look at each other.

Are we still best friends, are we still lovers?

Are we now tied to this emotional space?

Because we refuse to give up this race?

We've been asked, how do you keep the flame alive?

We don't just let it burn, we make it thrive.

Be sure to give it oxygen and let it breathe.

Then neither of you will want to leave.

Let the fire ignite your love but not consume,

Make sure you give each other plenty of room.

But not so much, that you don't feel the heat,

It's a daily balance of how your two souls meet.

We have a plan to make it last.

Every year we leave stuff in the past.

Some of the years exceeded the calendar's length.

Those were the years we really saw our strength.

Like every couple, we set out for forever.

We sealed our deal by agreeing to divorce never.

We continue to hang in there

Through thick and thin.

Because solo we are good

But we know together we win.

There will be disagreements,

With us being from Venus and Mars.

So take care of bumps becoming bruises

And bruises becoming scars.

We've stayed together, with trust and honesty,

From the start.

We're keeping our promise of till death do us part.

1 Corinthians and Me

Love has made a fool of me too many times to count,
But that doesn't mean I stop coming back for more.
With each encounter I learn something new.
I am the liar and love is the truth.

I keep blaming love for every mistake,
When really it's the choices I make.
I still have so much to learn,
Before love and I take another turn.

What I have found,
That has turned my thinking around,
Is that love doesn't hurt.
The one who doesn't know how to love
Hurts and gets hurt.

Love really is patient and kind,
I am not always either,
So I rush when I should wait and then I lash out.

Love does not envy or boast and is not proud;
The minute he does something extraordinary,
I'm singing like the little bird in warm cow shit.
The cat quietly ate that loud bird.

Love does not dishonor others
and is not self-seeking;
There were times I loved just because,
I missed being loved,
Not because I honored what I was being given.

Love is not easily angered
and keeps no record of wrongs,
If only it were as easy to forget the wrongs done.
This part of love is not the fun one.

Love does not delight in evil,
it rejoices with the truth.
This is the pureness of love that keeps me in pursuit.

Love protects, trusts, hopes, and perseveres,
Just like me
Apparently I am love, and I keep looking for myself.

I keep finding love but it doesn't stick with me.
Why is it that I seem to lack the key,
To unlock love and all of its treasure.
My love goals are consistent at every measure.

Is it because I'm a perverted, twisted, Christian, freak,
That I can't find the love that I seek?
Or is it because I haven't learned the lesson yet?
Love is about what you give, not just what you get.

To Have Lusted

Access

You want access:

Do you have a ticket?

Are you prepared to lick it?

Will you get on your knees?

And say pretty please?

You say you want access:

Can you plant your face?

All up in my vaginal space?

Will you kiss these lips?

While holding on to these hips?

You act like you want access:

Can you perform like a strong man?

Without using your hands?

Can you make your hard tongue swirl?

But lick me soft like a girl?

You touch me like you want access:

Are you trying to get me hot?

So I let you touch my spot?

Should I determine your technique?

Before we get between these sheets?

You stand there like you want access:

Or are you confused?

Is my show of power too much for you?

Should I tell you to go home

and let me take care of me alone?

Or should I invite you in and let you bring a friend?

If you're really sure, then this is where we begin.

Your access has been granted, so come on in.

Say yes

He called this morning to say he would be attending a conference half way between us in a few weeks. "Come stay with me", he said "I'll do the conference in the morning and you in the afternoon and again in the evening". The breathing is heavy on the phone, mine, not his. Everything I wanted to say about dating other people, the long distance causing a strain on us and the sexual frustration putting a strain on my battery supply, and the absence of his touch driving me insane and I say none of it because my brain is on pause.

Upon hearing his voice and his words, the only thing I can think about is getting done for 3 days straight! This man, this tall, dark, handsome, rugged, finely built man just curled my toes across this wireless air, so much so that I think my phone is overheating. Not only is he giving me an eargasm he's simultaneously sexting me, damn Bluetooth, I'm gonna lose it, right here at my desk! He just sent me a pic showing "My idea of breakfast in bed"…I like the way this man thinks. I told him that I would be his breakfast, brunch, lunch, dinner, and snack.

Now my mind is racing through the many times he's given me the gift of his tongue. Every time he eats me I feel like it's my birthday. This is not an exaggeration! He treats my clit like its ice cream on a cone, swirling, licking, and not letting a drip get away and then when I'm about to erupt he puts his whole mouth on it and nibbles. The first time he did that I told him to "stop showing off", turns out he wasn't showing off, that was just his basic meal. The deluxe meal has made me literally beg and I've never begged anyone, ever, until Him.

So between his milk chocolaty, silky smooth baritone in my ear telling me how much he wants to eat me and the picture of his cucumber thick and nearly foot-long dick in my mind, I am completely and utterly undone. All I can say is "YES".

Carnal Quickie

Hungry but I wanted him more than I wanted to eat.

Tired but I wanted him more than I wanted to sleep.

If I'm being honest with myself, I wanted him more than I wanted anything.

I have known it to be true that you cannot indulge more than one carnal desire at a time.

So as tired and hungry as I was, my flesh won out.

I needed to be fucked, more than rested or fed.

I'll eat later and I'll sleep when I'm dead.

I walked in his door to his awaiting arms.

He could tell I was tired but that raised no alarms.

I was on break before my next class.

So he grabbed me quickly and slapped my ass.

"Wake up" he said, "You're here".

The sound of his voice and the look in his eyes,

Is causing the temperature to rise
between my thighs.

I am fully awake and hungry for him.

I go to the wall and assume the position,

With no food or sleep, I'm on a mission.

Up goes my skirt and my ass is bare,

He's banging me hard and pulling my hair.

He's ready to feed me, I'm ready to swallow his load.

Energized and full now, time to hit the road.

FWB

Just the thought of you is making me wet

Spending lunch lingerie shopping on the net

Getting ready for our weekend ahead

We're finally going to get in the bed

All of this talking, this long foreplay

I'm ready for our roll in the hay

I have heard all about your moves

Trust me baby, I've got some too

I just want to crest this peak

We've been talking about

Show you what I can do with my mouth

Feel your tongue against my clit

Fuck me so hard, make it difficult to sit

I'm ready handsome, I've waited so long

To know how it feels to have you inside

These words, I just cannot describe

We're almost done waiting, the time is near

I can hear you whisper "I want you" in my ear

Driving me wild with our late night chats

Sexting and texting till we fall asleep

I'm always looking forward till next we speak

Are we going to do this

or just keep discussing this shit

Our friendship transition to friends with benefits

So enough with the talking it's time we fuck

We have to do it soon or we'll be Friend Zone stuck

3 date test

1st date – the height test: wear at least 3 inch heels on the first date, if he lied about his height, you will know

2nd date – the focus test: wear something very low cut, if he can still focus on the conversation instead of your girls, he gets a third date

3rd date – the rhythm test: go dancing or bowling, or something that requires movement, if

he's awkward with his body and/or can't keep a beat, it's a wrap. If you have no vertical rhythm your horizontal rhythm is likely to be off.

That is just the first round of testing.

There's the physical pre-sex tests, including the kiss test (self-explanatory), the touch test (does he know where to put his hands, again any awkwardness requires further examination), and the bare chest test (if he's hairy, do you like hairy, if he's bare do you prefer hairy). Also, let's not forget the Marcus (Eddie Murphy's Boomerang character) test. Are his feet a mess?

Of course, the biggest test of all is the sex test which often requires retesting, make-up testing, and an oral test. Yes you should grade on a curve because every new test taker must be compared to the most recent highest score! If he is at or near the bottom of the curve, he has failed the course and needs to be held back for further instruction. Now if he's a keeper, by that I mean "a quick learner", it might be worth it, but if not, DUMP HIM because no one has time for bad sex!!!!!!

Appetizer

His hands are in my hair caressing my scalp, kneading more and more with each stroke of my tongue as if he were preparing a loaf. His cranial massage is both tough and tender until he can take it no more.

He grabs my shoulders, I grab his ass, pulling him deeply into my wet mouth and I look up at him from under my eyelashes as he throws his head back and thrusts forward, I am rewarded for my efforts.

He lifts me to the dinner table. His appetizer is ready. He starts by nibbling my earlobes, then down to my neck, then my breast, first the right and then the slightly larger left.

While he is still feasting on my breasts his hand travels down my body and he uses his thumb to prime his meal, dessert he says, before dinner, as he heads south of my border.

I spread my legs giving him easier access to his meal, he brings his nose close, inhaling the aroma of musky anticipation. He kisses, then licks and sucks until he has caused such a flood of flavor that he can't help but lap at the spot of eruption, lest he drown. He marvels at my ability to repeatedly provide him with this nectar.

My juiciness has called him to attention again and he flips me over pressing my erect nipples against the cold hard table as he enters my warmth. He is so big and I fight to absorb his length and girth. His strong hands pressing down on my ample hips, he is grinding, pushing, stretching, expanding, and disappearing deeper and deeper into my body with the force of 10 men.

My entire body is screaming out in pleasure and pain, it hurts so good as he claims me by going full in, over and over again, forcing himself in and out of my body, he teases us both right to the edge and finally, he pushes us over the climax cliff and as the scream escapes my mouth, he leans over, laying light kisses all over my back, whispering in my ear, "you're mine" he says and calm overtakes me as the feeling of complete fullness shocks me into silence.

He sits at the table with me on his lap, still impaled. The timer goes off…dinner is ready.

Daydreaming

Daydreaming of last night...

The warmth of your body makes me shiver as the thought of that thing you did with your tongue, flows through my mind and my body responds as if you and I were still there on that oasis of serenity.

The music was low and slow in the background; I could hear nothing, but I could feel your touch as the flowers don't hear the wind but they feel the sun. Your hands were all over me and mine all over you, me, soft and wet, and you hard all over.

You stroking, kissing, licking all the way down to my toes and stopping half way back up to make sure I was wet enough. I began to shake and shiver but not from the cold.

Your entry was immediate, strong, thick, tight, and I struggled to adjust

Coitus Interrupter: "Don't stop" I whispered, and all you heard was don't, so you stopped.

BJ

The anticipation is building, I can hardly sit still

Can't wait to get my lips around your dick,

To smell your musky, manly scent,

As I make my descent

To my knees, to please you and me

See, I love it when you slip down my throat

Using your pre-cum to provide a coat

Of lubrication for my vocal cords

As I feel you swell in my mouth

I feel so in control of our pleasure

With every measured stroke in and out

Of my mouth, you pin my shoulders harder

To the wall, from down here you are so tall

And I feel so small compared to your largesse

My big man is ready to give me what I need

Taking the lead you fill my mouth

Shouting and shuddering and shaking

I am making you curse out loud because I just won't

Stop sucking your head like a vacuum,

I swallow as I attempt

To empty

you out,

Only when I know you can't take anymore,

Do I raise my knees off of the floor,

To go and close the door.

Lollipop

Apple, grape, or cherry flavor

Get it wet, prepare to savor

One last lick now grab the stick

And rub it on my nub

Open my lips a little bit

Stick out your tongue and find the clit

Now lick, lick, lick, lick

Taste my sweetness mixed with candy

This is when the lollipop comes in handy

Lick me then lick it, nibble it a little bit

Make your tongue go in and out

That's the rhythm I'm talking about

Press your lips against my lips

Hold on tightly to my hips

Give me a kiss on these upper lips, I want a taste too

You're nice and hard, let's see what a lollipop can do

But please don't rush, I need one more suck,
before we fuck

Do that thing with the pressure and swirl

That arches my back and makes my toes curl

Ooo now my pussy is as sweet as can be

Dripping with natural nectar from me

I know you're ready to insert your dick

And get your ass pumping quick

But I just had the best climax

I need a few seconds to relax

Race

As soon as we got in the door he had me out of my
bottom layers, I hate winter he says as he pulls off
my skirt, boots, socks, tights, and thong. With half of
me exposed he bends me over the short wall and
starts going to town banging me from behind. I hold
onto the bowl of keys with one hand and the wall
with the other as his quick but deep thrusts literally
have me on my toes. He's tall and I'm not, so he lifts
my legs and before I know it I'm a slightly tilted
wheelbarrow and I can feel him against my back
wall which really gets my juices flowing. Inverted
like this he's slamming into my g-spot and I can't
help but scream as I climax for the first time tonight.

I'm hot now so off with the sweater, shirt, camisole
and bra. I back up into his groin until he is at the

edge of the steps. I spin around and drop to my knees, now he's the one holding onto the wall. I take him into my wet mouth, tasting my juices all over him. I'm stroking, licking, sucking, and using one hand to torque his shaft while fingering his gouch with the other. I'm blowing hot air kisses up and down his long length and I continue to push him deeper down my throat past my gag reflex until his balls are grazing my cheeks and he keeps saying "O shit". I'm breathing through my nose and taking a deep breathe I let out a long hum through my mouth. The vibrations it creates for him makes him weak in the knees. He can't sing but I swear I hear him belt out six different octaves of "O shit". That last gruff one means he's done. He pulls me to my feet by my hair and now we are one for one, a climax tie.

He lifts me up into his arms and I wrap my legs

around him. He carries me upstairs to the bed. He's still holding me in his arms while he pulls back the cover and places me gently on the bed. It is the most tender he's been this evening and I know what's coming.

He lays perpendicular to me with his head in my lap. He lifts one of my legs and turns his torso toward my head and I am trapped by his body and his tongue. His soft hair feels like silk in my hands and I stroke as he strokes. The pleasure is excruciating. He has me right where he wants me and I cannot get him in my mouth in this position but I can jerk him until he is at full attention again. I am pinned down and he is torturing my clit while he flicks and plucks and nibbles until I am begging him to put his tongue right there...and then he goes all in, using his deft fingers to open me up and his tongue feels thick and strong and with one last flick I go over the edge. He flattens his tongue against my opening and I climax for the second time. He doesn't stop. He lifts my leg higher and opens me wider and continues to swirl his tongue around the tender nerve endings at the opening of my vagina until I am bucking and gyrating and fucking his tongue like there's no tomorrow and here I go again. I think he wants me to win. My three to his one.

I am spent but he doesn't let me rest. He turns me over and shifts himself and now we're on our sides, head to feet, and my legs are around his neck, and he's spooning me from behind and I feel his length pressing against my backdoor. At this point I already know that walking will be a sacrifice tomorrow. He's prodding me open and I'm looking down into his eyes and he's waiting for my affirmative response. I arch my back and lift my leg to let him in, I bite down on my lip as he pushes past my anal sphincter. He's going up where the design is for down. It's so tight in reverse. He is patient while I wait for my pain relays to calm down and I relax my muscles and then he starts a slow in and out rhythm. He holds onto my hip from above and my inner leg from below, using his thumb pad to massage my soaking wet pussy and he is kissing the inside of my calf resting next to his face while his speed increases, distracting me and keeping me relaxed. Wait, what is happening here? He's massaging my hip while he's fucking me in the ass. I am overwhelmed and bewildered by the onslaught of sensations coursing through my body right now, pain, pleasure, discomfort, relaxation; I am contorted, and stretched out. His hands are everywhere until finally he grabs my hip and he climaxes, tenderly and quietly. He massages my ass as he pulls out slowly, pain management. Three to two, he's gaining on me.

I rest while he goes to clean up. He returns with a cloth, water, and towel and he bathes me protecting us both from any transfer. We lay closely together to warm up after our temperature drop. Soon we are entangled bodies and tongues, heating up our flesh and the room. I have closed the space between us within minutes by wrapping my trained dancer's leg around his torso and lowering myself onto him as we lay side to side. He loves my flexibility. When I'm open wide like this he can get balls deep and I am completely filled by his length and thickness. He pulls out to the tip and then thrusts back in, slow, shallow, slow, shallow and then fast and deep, it's a game he plays. We cannot get enough of each other in this position. Face to face we can see the pleasure in each other's reflections. All of my senses are alive. I see his handsome face, the room has the distinct scent of sex, I still taste me on his lips; we are exploring each other's touch, and then I hear it, the impending explosion, that rumbling, like a train coming down the tracks, down from my toes, up to my head, and he's there with me, neck and neck, we are pushing each other. He's stroking me and I tighten my pelvic muscles around him and we go back and forth and back and forth, holding on tightly to one another as we can feel that it's so close, until we collapse in a heap of flesh, crossing the finish line together. Four to three final score. We are both winners.

Proposition

Sometimes I'm just too sassy, for my own damn good
But I won't tone it down, though maybe I should

It probably starts too soon
for the owner of a conventional mind
You need to know what you're getting into
trust me, I'm being kind

Friend or more, you need to be sure
before you choose a side
There are no brakes no airbags or seat belts
on this sexy ride

It's good to see that you're open-minded
and fearless like me
Now that you've chosen to be more
let me give you the key

Knocking before entry is the way to open every door
But once inside there's no need for keeping score

I will tell you the same as I've told the others before
Just because I love to fuck does not make me a whore

Don't treat me like one and we'll get along just fine
Come sit close to me and we'll listen to Ginuwine

Time to strap up, I'm ready to ride your "Pony" now
Side saddle, cowgirl, and bareback, that's how

We don't need a ring, or a church ceremony
I'm not here trying to collect alimony

I just want us to share
our hearts, souls, and bodies
in ecstasy
An exhilarating exchange of pleasure
between you and me

A physical apology

Rough hands on my smooth skin causing my nerve endings to stir as he pushes his tongue past my lips with mint flavored kisses and his 5 o'clock shadow harsh against my tender labret causing the early stars of twilight to dance beneath my lids.

Everything moves so fast in slow motion, clothing removed at the speed of sound, my satin fibers gliding across his natural cotton until we are rubbing skin against skin in a delicate torture, increasing room and body temperatures.

This naked dance of heated, hot, nasty kisses, licking sweat to satisfy our thirst from the days of the dry, barren, parched landscape of our bodies. We use our mouths to increase lubrication to reduce the impending friction.

Days of soundless interaction are now a crescendo of lust until the pounding of the blood flow in my ears is deafening, the scream upon entry and the hammering of every thrust is so loud when bodies are under construction, building a climax is not silent work.

Just like that, everything is reset, a temporary impasse to an otherwise uneventful day, two frustrated people going on their way, conflict resolution at its finest, solutions provided with no allocutions.

Physical connection is sometimes all that is needed to really say,

I'm sorry.

Penetration

At the end of date one, thoughts of you keep
penetrating my mind. After dinner I was unable to
think of anything but having you inside of me. We
sat on the same side of the table your leg against my
leg, sending electrical pulses down to my toes. Your
hand brushed against my thigh, burning through my
skirt leaving an imprint I refuse to remove. Your
sexy baritone penetrated my sound barrier all night;
following me home and into bed, narrating my
explicitly restrictive NC-17 dreams. Too soon.

At the end of date two, we had that first real kiss.
When your tongue penetrated my mouth it was
everything I knew it would be, hot, steamy, probing,
and wet. You held me to you with your hand on the
back of my neck, dominating but not aggressive. I
sucked on your bottom lip and you licked every inch
of my oral cavity. We stood at my door for what
seemed like hours, exploring, penetrating each other,
over and over again. I was so heated as I stepped
inside and headed to the shower to cool off. Your wet

kisses on my wet skin are what I really wanted. Really, too soon.

At the end of date three I let you come inside. We talked late into the night, you began to penetrate my heart. We kissed again and touched even more starting at second base. Then we had a few nightcaps before rounding third. You slipped two fingers inside of me, measuring my width while I did the same unable to fit you inside my fist. I thought, this is going to be great when it finally happens. You quickly changed up the game and lifted my skirt, pushing my panties aside; you penetrated me with your tongue to my utter inebriated surprise. It felt so good that I screamed out loud when you and I were done. You kissed and bit the insides of my legs, your teeth penetrating my skin. Still, too soon.

At the end of date four, we are sitting on your couch. I can't believe you cooked dinner for us. A manly man who knows his way around the kitchen; I am impressed by your finesse. I know why I am here. I'm ready for the main penetration. I wore pretty panties and a matching bra tonight. You want to talk about it first, so you start by penetrating my mind. Have I heard of Kama Sutra? Do I like it fast and hard? Do I like being tied up? Is it ok if you spank my ass? Do I like it from behind? How do I feel about being on top? You want to know my comfort zone. I say yes to everything and anything else that you think to ask. You have penetrated all of my defenses and my gates have flung open wide. You take me to your bedroom and penetrate me repeatedly throughout the night. In the morning we had sex for breakfast. It was over, too soon.

Reconnection

My body has been screaming for the last three
weeks, give me some, get some, find some now

My hands are cramping and I am out of batteries

My brain is distracted by every single horny thought

My eyes deceive me when I see penis instead of pants
and blowjob instead of blowout

My mind reads fuck and suck not dockers and
hairdryers

My face is breaking out with hormone overloads

My skin is desperate for foreign touch

My own hands' caress is simply not enough

My willpower is weak, must get some, find some,
have some now

My every step, feels like a hundred miles

My heart is heavy with his distance

My nose can no longer remember his scent

My lips miss being wrapped around his manhood

My inner voice pleads incessantly louder, and
louder, give me some, get some, find some now

My ears yearn to hear him whisper
take it, have it, here it is

I can no longer do this on my own

I crave him to make it right

I want him to take me, make me, do me now

I need school to be out and work to be on hold

I wish for a holly jolly holiday to make it all ok

I long to get some, find some, have some now

I will run, bike, and swim with triathlon records
to break this fast

I should be eaten out, flipped over and jammed

I keep thinking about having my itch scratched

I believe him when he says, soon baby soon

I know how it goes, how it feels and how it works

I have to get some, find some, have some now

I am ready to get on my knees and please

I do not need conversation, I only need his
participation

I have arrived, it is the time
to get some, give some, have some now

We kiss at the door and head upstairs

We leave a Hansel and Gretel trail
of clothing on our way

We only expose the important parts,
time is not on our side

We have to get some, give some, have some now

We go at each other, like anxious wrestlers,
half-naked wrestlers

We nibble, suck, kiss, touch and stroke

We can barely breathe
yet we refuse to come up for air

We burn our tongues on each other's skin

We hastily throw our bodies, one against the other

We must get some, give some, take some now

We bang, he thrusts, I buck my hips

We dance horizontally across the bed

We leave no part untouched, unkissed, unloved

We give each other everything

We had some, we got some,

We're going to get some more,

later.

Mr. Responsible

We were both frustrated as he dressed for an unexpected Saturday at the office. We had planned to make love all day and now I was being left alone with my toys, while he went off to discuss torts with other equally sexually frustrated men.

Our plans to screw all day were screwed but I wanted to send him off right so he would hurry home, but he wouldn't let me touch him, "I'm already late", he said. "Just a taste baby", I said, but he would not be deterred. "Someone has to be the responsible one" he said, "If I'm not there they won't get it done right." "Fine" I said, "you go be Mr. Responsible and I'll see you for lunch".

Just because he wanted to be the "responsible one" didn't mean I had to join the sexually frustrated party, so before I hit the shower I stopped at the bed and whipped out one of my toys and started to play as he attempted to get dressed.

I began enjoying my toy and ignoring the frustration of not being able to touch him like I wanted. My body was heating up so I turned up the intensity. The pulsating rhythm increased, I started moaning and groaning as my body writhed against my battery operated beast.

Mr. Responsible was at the closet door mirror tying his tie, a task he usually accomplishes in under a minute was taking ten. I know he was watching me get there on vibrations not provided by his tongue and he just could not look away.

I was losing control, bucking, kicking, arching my back, thrashing around the bed, touching my breast, my hips, my lips, with my free hand until my entire body shook and shuddered taking me to the top of my toe-curling, juice flowing, erotic climax. I lay there spent in pure ecstasy, body glistening and fully satisfied. Remembering I was not alone, I finally looked up to find him staring at me, wide-eyed. It looked like he was trying to say something but no sound escaped his opened mouth. I smiled a wicked smile and licked my lips. I'd never seen this loquacious lawyer lover of mine without words.

Mr. Responsible just stood there as I strutted up to him on my way to the shower. I made sure my erect nipples pressed into his hard chest as I leaned in and whispered in his ear. "I'm going to take a quick shower but you might want to re-button your shirt and put on matching socks." and then I left him standing there.

I could hear a flurry of activity behind me as I turned the water on in the shower. He'll be here in 4, 3, 2, 1...Mr. Responsible my ass.

To all these young bucks hitting on me

These little boys still playing with toys

Measuring their dicks and sending me pics

Don't they know it's not about the size of the ship

But the experience of the captain

who can make the clit flip

Can you set a course and reach the G spot

Or are you still wet behind the ears trying to plot

A way to get a suga mamma to pay your bills

I don't need a boy, I need a grown man with skills

You say you've got a young back

You don't need a blue pill

Is that all you think is required to seal this deal

You must have finesse and some hair on your chest

The ability to make me yell while you exorcise my
demons, keep me cumming and keep me screaming

I think you might be carried away
with all of that MILF dreaming

You talk a lot but is your game on point

Can you suck it, lick it, flick it and then stick it
or are you just trying to hit it

Run along little boy and learn how to dance,
step aside and make room for a real man

I see you puffing out your chest
trying to establish your manliness
You have no understanding
of this grown folk business

I am an experienced woman in my sexual prime,
not some little girl,

Yet somehow you think you're man enough,
to really rock my world

So come on young man, let me see what you've got
My time is valuable but perhaps yours is not

O performance anxiety or is it too cold,
Or really is it just that I'm too bold

See you're really not ready for all that I have,
Why don't you go on home and send me your dad!

One day will you

One day when you are old,
will you remember that you were bold?
Will you tell the ones that come behind you,
all that you used to be?

One day when you are not young anymore,
will you tell your grown children
that you were a Slore?
Will you tell the ones that come behind you,
all that you used to do?

One day when your end is near,
will you say how often your legs were in the air?
Will you tell the ones that come behind you,
the number of partners you had?

One day when all of your freaky friends are gone,
will you be satisfied climaxing alone?
Will you tell the ones that come behind you,
how often you applied self-care?

One day when your multiple curves are one,
will you look at your pics and remember the fun?
Will you tell the ones that come behind you,
how hot your body was?

One day when you need help to stay wet,
will you remember how juicy you used to get?
Will you tell the ones that come behind you,
how easily excited you got?

Will you tell the ones that come behind you,
that you were a hot sexpot?
Will you tell the ones that come behind you,
how sad you are that age made it stop?

Will you tell the ones that come behind you all of
that? Well maybe not

But one day when you lay dying,
when all the ones that come behind you are crying,
will your libido finally quit trying?

I certainly hope not.

2 for Me

He starts with his hands on my back, I've told him how much I like that.

Massaging my shoulders, relaxing me, I lean into his stance as he warms my body.

He wraps one arm around the front while using the other to continue rubbing my back.

Caressing my breast, traveling down my abs, and feeling around my small waist.

She's watching us, paying close attention, she wants in on the massage.

Soon I am seated between them and the kissing and caressing are non-stop.

The room is warm, close to hot, I begin to melt.

I now know how Katy Perry felt, I'm kissing a girl and I like it, soft, gentle, flaming hot kisses.

I am being kissed front and back and there are hands everywhere,

Like that four hands massage I had once while on vacation, it is a feeling of pure bliss.

All of my nerve endings are on alert and I can hardly contain the quivering.

So this is happening, the next step of my sexual evolution is here...

His finger and her tongue are on me. He is guiding her, teaching her, how to bring me pleasure.

Her tongue is smaller than I'm used to but doesn't necessarily feel different, still wet, still focused.

I am not sure which of us is more excited by this change of position and perspective.

She is eager to learn, he is eager to teach, and I am just eager.

After she learns how to get my body to respond by the angle of her tongue on my clit, her first lesson is done.

He is obviously more experienced and she returns to kissing me while he uses his hand to help me reach climax and as I moan into her mouth, he kisses my back. Unbefuckinglievable.

It felt like an hour but really, ten minutes ago he was out on the deck grilling and she and I were watching tv.

The Duds

There was a man I loved so much
We had so much in common
But he could not eat me well
And that became a problem

Another guy I rushed to meet
Was a nasty freak between the sheets
Liked to lick my ass when we were done
But a big dick isn't much fun
When the owner is also one

I wasn't attracted to any white guys
My blackness offered me so many lies
Until I met one who really rocked my world
But then I learned he was doing that
With two other girls

And then I sank so very low
Because of his hot body and me being a ho
He was the scarecrow from the Wiz,
some men, I just can't train

I am still ashamed till this day,
that I fucked a guy without a brain

The worst was with the average Joe

That had good equipment but just didn't know

How to really hit that spot

He bored me to death so I had to stop

Finally there was the one who lied

Made me take measures to protect his pride

Because he was the nicest guy, I really really tried

But sadly there was just not enough size

So I gave an Oscar worthy performance and…cried

So yes I've had a lot of it,

but all of it wasn't the best

It's simply trial and error

to separate the Duds from the rest

I've Had Good

I've had good sex. I mean reeeeeeally good sex. I'm talking about toe-curling, eye rolling, consciousness losing, coming to on the floor of the bedroom closet, good sex.

I've had good sex with boys and good sex with men and experience does not necessarily come with age, at least not when it comes to sex. I've had good sex while in love and good sex while not, and love does not make sex better, sex makes love better.

I've had good sex. Lots of different experiences of really good sex. Variety is the spice of a good sex life. I don't mean a variety of partners, I'm not that kind of girl. I mean a variety of position, of speed, of rhythm, of force, of lighting, of mood, of day, of place, of length, of amount... well you get the picture. Can the same two people enjoy that much variety? Sure! It's the *other* stuff that determines the success or failure of the relationship. I have never heard of a couple breaking up because the sex was um...too good.

I've had good sex. I've had really good, make a porn star blush, sex. I've had naughty, freaky, spank me, slap your mama, good sex. Dress up sex: I've been the cheerleader, the school girl, the hot teacher, and the policewoman with tie me up, tie me down sex. Don't just fantasize! Be the fantasy, live the fantasy, and soon the fantasy is your reality.

I've had good sex. I've had stay in the bed all weekend sex. I've had don't eat, don't sleep, just have sex all day and night, sex. I've had break the bed, scratch the walls, damage the floor, shatter the earth, good sex. I've had can't walk straight, can't sit down, send me spinning, put my vortex out of commission, sex. I've had some really, really good sex. In fact I think I'll go have some right now.

About the Author

I chase technology, numbers, and two amazing teenagers in my everyday life but my Facebook post from August 7, 2009 tells you exactly who I am: I can't do it all, I can't have it all, I don't know it all and I'm good with that. I do what I can, I have what I need, and I'm learning everyday – contentment. I continue to strive to do more, I know desire is not necessity and I still want, and the quest for knowledge is never ending – ambition. I was, I am, I will be – growth...always evolving. Move, live, love, laugh, and learn, lest all you do is grow...old.

Thanks for reading.